CRYPTIDS OF THE COAST

CRYPTIDS OF THE COAST

THOMAS SHELTON

CONTENTS

CHAPTER 1

Introduction to Cadborosaurus

Origin of the Cadborosaurus Legend

The Cadborosaurus legend originates from the coastal waters of the Pacific Northwest, particularly around the Gulf Islands of British Columbia and Washington State. First reported by Indigenous peoples long before European contact, this enigmatic creature has been described in various forms, often resembling a long-necked marine reptile or a serpent-like entity. Historical accounts suggest that sightings date back to the early 19th century, with many Indigenous narratives painting the creature as a protector of the sea, thus intertwining local mythology with the natural world. The integration of these ancient stories into contemporary cryptozoological discourse highlights the enduring fascination with Cadborosaurus and its place in the cultural landscape.

Eyewitness accounts of Cadborosaurus have proliferated since the 1930s, with numerous sightings reported by fishermen, sailors, and local residents. Each story contributes to the evolving legend, detailing the creature's size, shape, and behavior. Some witnesses describe a large, undulating body, while others emphasize its long neck and horse-like head. These varying descriptions reflect not only individual perceptions but also the influence of local folklore and environmental factors. As the legend grew, so did the interest in collecting these narratives, leading to a more structured approach in documenting sightings and the people behind them.

Scientific studies surrounding the Cadborosaurus legend have sought to explore both the biological possibilities and the ecological implications of such a creature existing in the coastal waters of North America. Researchers have examined the potential for undiscovered marine species, drawing parallels with known animals like the oarfish or the basking shark, which could be misidentified by observers. Additionally, the environmental impact on the habitats that might support such creatures remains a topic of interest. Investigating factors such as water temperature, prey availability, and ocean currents contributes to a broader understanding of the ecosystem where Cadborosaurus is said to reside.

The Cadborosaurus has also found its way into popular culture and media, becoming a symbol of mystery and intrigue. Documentaries, books, and television series have explored its legend, often blending scientific inquiry with sensational storytelling. Artistic interpretations of Cadborosaurus, ranging from sketches to digital illustrations, have further fueled public interest, creating a visual mythology that captivates imaginations. These representations often reflect the cultural context of their creation, showcasing how the legend has evolved alongside advancements in media and technology.

The ongoing exploration of Cadborosaurus is not just a quest for a mythical creature but also an investigation into the nature of belief and the human desire for discovery. Comparisons with other sea monsters, such as the Loch Ness Monster or the Kraken, reveal a shared fascination with the unknown that transcends geographical boundaries. As cryptozoologists continue their search, the interplay between historical accounts, scientific inquiry, and cultural narratives will shape the future of the Cadborosaurus legend, ensuring its place in the annals of cryptozoological study and the collective imagination of coastal communities.

The Coastal Habitat of Cadborosaurus

The coastal habitat of Cadborosaurus, believed to inhabit the waters off the Pacific Northwest, is a critical area for understanding this elusive cryptid. It is characterized by a rich array of marine ecosystems that provide both sustenance and shelter for a variety of species. From the kelp forests along the shore to the deep waters of the continental shelf, these environments create an ideal backdrop for the existence of a large sea creature. The diversity of marine life, including fish, crustaceans, and marine mammals, suggests that Cadborosaurus, if it exists, would have ample food sources to support its survival.

Eyewitness accounts of Cadborosaurus often describe it in close proximity to coastal regions, particularly around bays and estuaries. These areas are known for their complex ecosystems where freshwater meets saltwater, creating a unique environment teeming with life. Sightings frequently occur during periods of calm weather or in the early morning when the waters are less disturbed. Such conditions not only increase visibility but may also affect the behavior of marine creatures, potentially bringing Cadborosaurus closer to the surface. Analyzing these sightings provides valuable insights into the creature's habits and preferences regarding its habitat.

Scientific studies and theories surrounding Cadborosaurus often delve into its potential ecological niche. Some researchers propose that this creature could be a surviving member of a prehistoric marine reptile, akin to the plesiosaurs. Others suggest that it might be a previously unknown species of large marine animal, adapted to its coastal environment. Understanding the habitat requirements of such an organism is essential for evaluating the plausibility of its existence. Research into similar marine habitats and their inhabitants can yield clues about the ecological dynamics that would support a creature like Cadborosaurus.

In popular culture, Cadborosaurus has become emblematic of the mysteries that coastal waters hold. Documentaries, books, and artistic interpretations frequently draw upon the allure of this cryptid, weaving narratives that highlight both the scientific and folkloric elements of its story. These portrayals often reflect the fascination with the unknown and the human desire to connect with nature's mysteries. As a result, the coastal habitat of Cadborosaurus not only serves as a physical setting but also as a canvas for artistic expression and storytelling, enriching the cultural significance of the cryptid.

Environmental impacts on the coastal habitats of Cadborosaurus are critical to consider in the ongoing search for this creature. Coastal development, pollution, and climate change pose significant threats to these ecosystems, potentially affecting the availability of prey and suitable living conditions. As cryptozoology enthusiasts continue to investigate the existence of Cadborosaurus, understanding these environmental factors becomes increasingly important. Protecting these coastal habitats may not only help preserve the biodiversity of the region but could also play a vital role in safeguarding the legacy of Cadborosaurus, ensuring that future generations can explore the mysteries of this enigmatic creature.

CHAPTER 2

Eyewitness Accounts

Notable Sightings Through the Years

Notable sightings of Cadborosaurus throughout the years have intrigued cryptozoologists and casual observers alike, prompting a blend of skepticism and fascination. The first recorded sighting dates back to the late 19th century, when a local fisherman in Cadboro Bay, British Columbia, reported encountering an enormous serpent-like creature. This initial account laid the groundwork for the legend of Cadborosaurus, capturing the attention of both the public and researchers. Over the decades, various sightings have emerged, each adding to the tapestry of reports surrounding this elusive marine cryptid.

Throughout the 20th century, numerous eyewitness accounts contributed to the growing lore of Cadborosaurus. In the 1930s, a group of children playing on the beach claimed to have seen a long, undulating creature swimming just offshore. Their descriptions, along with sketches they provided, sparked interest among local researchers. These accounts often characterized the creature as having a long neck and multiple humps, solidifying its image as a sea serpent in the minds of many. Such sightings prompted scientific inquiries, although definitive evidence remained elusive, leading to ongoing debates about the creature's existence.

The 1990s saw a resurgence in Cadborosaurus sightings, notably when a group of kayakers off the coast of Vancouver Island reported a massive creature breaching the surface of the water. Their detailed descriptions, coupled with the proliferation of video technology, fueled discussions within the cryptozoology community. Documentaries produced during this period aimed to explore these claims, featuring interviews with eyewitnesses and analyses of historical reports. These films not only popularized the mystery of Cadborosaurus but also encouraged a new generation of enthusiasts to take an interest in marine cryptids.

Comparisons between Cadborosaurus and other legendary sea monsters have also emerged as a focal point in discussions of its existence. Similarities to creatures like the Loch Ness Monster and the Nile's Serpent have prompted examination of how folklore shapes our understanding of marine life. While skeptics argue that sightings can often be attributed to misidentified marine animals or natural phenomena, proponents of Cadborosaurus continue to advocate for its existence based on the patterns in historical accounts and modern sightings. This ongoing debate emphasizes the complexities of cryptozoology as a field of study.

Artistic interpretations of Cadborosaurus have flourished alongside these sightings, further embedding the creature into popular culture. Illustrations ranging from fearsome depictions to more whimsical renditions have captured the imagination of both the public and researchers. This artistic representation not only reflects the cultural significance of the creature but also serves as a means of preserving its legacy. As environmental changes impact marine habitats, the survival of Cadborosaurus, whether real or metaphorical, becomes intertwined with the larger narrative of ocean conservation and the mysteries that still lie beneath the waves.

Analysis of Eyewitness Credibility

The credibility of eyewitness accounts plays a crucial role in the study of cryptids like Cadborosaurus, particularly given the creature's elusive nature. Eyewitness testimonies often form the backbone of evidence for its existence, yet they must be approached with a critical lens. Factors such as the psychological state of the observer, environmental conditions at the time of the sighting, and the potential for misidentifications can significantly influence the reliability of these accounts. Understanding these elements allows cryptozoologists to assess the validity of reports and separate genuine encounters from those that may be more fanciful or erroneous.

Research into the psychology of perception reveals that human memory is not as infallible as we might believe. Eyewitnesses may unknowingly distort their recollections due to stress, excitement, or suggestion. In the case of Cadborosaurus sightings, witnesses often describe a large, serpentine creature, yet the interpretation of what they see can vary widely. Factors such as lighting, distance, and the observer's prior knowledge of marine life can lead to different conclusions about what was actually witnessed. This variability necessitates a careful examination of each account, with an emphasis on corroborating details that can lend credibility to the reports.

In addition to psychological factors, environmental influences are pivotal in evaluating eyewitness accounts of Cadborosaurus. The coastal waters of the Pacific Northwest, where sightings are most frequently reported, are known for their challenging visibility and dynamic conditions. Fog, choppy waters, and the presence of marine debris can all contribute to misinterpretations of what is seen. Cryptozoologists must therefore consider these environmental elements when analyzing sightings, as they can either enhance the mystery surrounding Cadborosaurus or clarify misunderstandings about its existence.

Scientific studies play an essential role in analyzing eyewitness credibility by providing a framework for understanding the biological and ecological contexts of reported sightings. Field research, coupled with data collection on local marine life, can help identify whether witnesses might have mistaken known species for Cadborosaurus. By comparing eyewitness descriptions with documented marine animals, researchers can determine patterns of misidentification and refine the search for the elusive creature. This scientific approach not only lends credibility to the field of cryptozoology but also helps establish a more rigorous methodology for future investigations.

Ultimately, the interplay of eyewitness credibility, environmental factors, and scientific inquiry shapes the narrative surrounding Cadborosaurus. As cryptozoology enthusiasts continue to explore this enigmatic creature, it is essential to maintain a balance between open-mindedness and skepticism. Engaging with eyewitness accounts while applying critical analysis can lead to a deeper understanding of both the phenomenon of Cadborosaurus and the broader implications it holds for the study of cryptids. This nuanced approach fosters a richer dialogue within the cryptozoology community, encouraging ongoing exploration and investigation into the mysteries of our natural world.

Patterns in Sightings

Patterns in sightings of Cadborosaurus reveal intriguing trends that can offer insights into the behaviors and habitats of this elusive creature. Eyewitness accounts often describe similar physical characteristics, such as a long neck, large body, and undulating movement in water. These recurring details suggest that many sightings may stem from a common source, possibly indicating a consistent type of creature that has been observed across various locations along the coast. The geographical distribution of reports often clusters around specific areas, such as the waters of British Columbia and the Gulf Islands, hinting at favored habitats where Cadborosaurus may thrive.

Moreover, the timing of sightings can provide additional context for understanding Cadborosaurus behavior. Many reports coincide with seasonal changes, particularly during warmer months when marine life is more abundant. This correlation raises questions about the creature's feeding patterns and migratory behaviors. Observers frequently note increases in sightings during late spring and summer, suggesting that Cadborosaurus may be more active during these periods, possibly due to the availability of prey or favorable environmental conditions.

Eyewitness accounts also highlight a range of emotional responses, from awe to fear, which can influence the credibility of the reports. Many witnesses describe a sense of wonder at encountering such a mysterious creature, while others express skepticism about their own perceptions. The psychological factors at play in these encounters are significant, as they can shape how sightings are reported and recorded. This underscores the importance of considering the human element in the study of cryptids, as personal beliefs and cultural backgrounds can impact the interpretation of an experience.

Scientific studies and theories surrounding Cadborosaurus often attempt to reconcile these patterns with known marine biology. Researchers explore the possibility that Cadborosaurus could be a surviving species of prehistoric marine reptile or a misidentified creature, such as a large seal or whale. Comparative analysis with documented marine life enables scientists to formulate hypotheses about the creature's potential existence. This intersection of folklore and science fuels ongoing debates within the cryptozoological community, as enthusiasts seek to validate or refute the existence of Cadborosaurus through empirical evidence.

In popular culture, the fascination with Cadborosaurus has inspired artistic interpretations and illustrations that further perpetuate the creature's mythos. Documentaries and media portrayals often dramatize eyewitness accounts, contributing to the sensationalism surrounding sightings. As a result, the narrative of Cadborosaurus continues to evolve, influenced by both historical folklore and contemporary interpretations. Engaging with these patterns in sightings not only enriches our understanding of Cadborosaurus but also highlights the enduring allure of cryptids within the broader landscape of marine mysteries.

CHAPTER 3

Scientific Studies and Theories

Biological Possibilities for Cadborosaurus

The possibility of the existence of Cadborosaurus, a reputed sea serpent inhabiting the waters off the coasts of British Columbia and Washington State, raises intriguing questions about its biological plausibility. Eyewitness accounts describe this creature as a long, serpent-like being, with a horse-like head and various features reminiscent of both reptiles and mammals. Such characteristics invite speculation about its potential classification within the existing biological taxonomy. Some cryptozoologists theorize that Cadborosaurus could be a surviving species of a prehistoric marine reptile, akin to the Plesiosaur, which might have adapted to contemporary ocean environments.

The habitat of Cadborosaurus presents another layer of complexity in understanding its biological possibilities. The coastal waters of the Pacific Northwest are rich in biodiversity, offering a variety of ecological niches. The deep, cold waters, combined with the presence of kelp forests and underwater topography, create ideal conditions for a large marine creature. These environments could support a creature of significant size, as the abundance of prey such as fish and other marine animals would provide a sustainable food source. Furthermore, the vastness of these waters allows for the possibility of large, elusive creatures remaining undetected by modern science.

The biological characteristics attributed to Cadborosaurus in eyewitness reports also suggest various adaptations that could facilitate survival in its marine environment. The creature's long body might imply a streamlined shape, beneficial for efficient movement through water. Its reported horse-like head could suggest specialized feeding adaptations, potentially allowing it to hunt a diverse range of prey. Additionally, the possibility of a layer of blubber or scales could provide insulation in colder waters, supporting the hypothesis that Cadborosaurus is well-suited to its habitat.

Comparisons with other cryptids and historical sea monsters further enrich the discussion on the biological possibilities of Cadborosaurus. The similarities it shares with known species such as the Giant Squid or the elusive Greenland Shark highlight the potential for undiscovered marine life. These creatures demonstrate that the ocean still holds mysteries that defy conventional understanding. Historical accounts and folklore surrounding sea monsters often describe beings that share traits with Cadborosaurus, lending credence to the idea that such creatures could exist, influenced by exaggerated tales of real animals.

Despite the challenges faced by cryptozoologists in substantiating the existence of Cadborosaurus, ongoing scientific studies and environmental assessments continue to explore the implications of its potential existence. These efforts not only aim to validate eyewitness accounts but also to understand the ecological dynamics of the regions where sightings occur. As technology advances, so does the ability to survey ocean depths more thoroughly, providing hope for capturing evidence of this enigmatic creature. The intersection of folklore, science, and public fascination with Cadborosaurus keeps the search alive, inviting both skepticism and wonder in the quest for understanding this elusive marine legend.

The Role of Marine Biology in Understanding

Marine biology plays a crucial role in understanding the enigmatic creature known as Cadborosaurus, often referred to as Caddy. This purported sea serpent has been the subject of fascination and speculation for decades, particularly among cryptozoology enthusiasts. By studying marine ecosystems and the species that inhabit them, marine biologists can provide insights into the potential existence of Cadborosaurus and its ecological niche. Investigating the biodiversity of coastal waters, including the presence of large marine animals and their behaviors, can inform theories about how a creature like Cadborosaurus might survive in the modern ocean.

Eyewitness accounts and sightings of Cadborosaurus often describe a creature that resembles both a serpent and a dinosaur, raising questions about its physical characteristics and behavior. Marine biology offers a framework for understanding these descriptions by comparing them to known marine species. For instance, the size and movement patterns of marine mammals, such as sea lions or large fish, can help assess whether sightings could be misidentifications of these animals. Additionally, examining the habitats where sightings occur can reveal whether conditions are conducive to supporting a large, elusive creature.

Scientific studies focused on marine habitats provide valuable context for understanding the potential environmental impacts on Cadborosaurus populations. Changes in water temperature, pollution, and fishing practices can significantly affect the ecosystems that might sustain such a creature. Marine biologists investigate these factors to ascertain whether they could contribute to the decline or disappearance of Cadborosaurus. By understanding these environmental pressures, enthusiasts can better comprehend the challenges that any elusive marine cryptid would face in today's oceans.

The cultural significance of Cadborosaurus is evident in its representation across various media, from documentaries to artistic illustrations. Marine biology not only enriches these representations but also grounds them in scientific reality. Documentaries that explore the possibility of Cadborosaurus often include interviews with marine biologists who discuss the feasibility of such a creature existing. Furthermore, artistic interpretations of Cadborosaurus can be informed by the anatomical features of real marine animals, providing a more realistic portrayal that resonates with both scientific inquiry and cryptozoological interest.

Lastly, the comparisons drawn between Cadborosaurus and other legendary sea monsters highlight the necessity of a marine biological perspective. By examining other documented marine species, such as the Loch Ness Monster or the

Ogopogo, researchers can identify common traits and behaviors that may also apply to Cadborosaurus. This comparative analysis not only strengthens the arguments for or against the existence of cryptids but also emphasizes the importance of marine biology in unraveling the mysteries of the ocean. Ultimately, the intersection of marine biology and cryptozoology can enhance our understanding of Cadborosaurus and its place in both scientific discourse and cultural lore.

Skepticism and Critique of Evidence

Skepticism plays a crucial role in the study of cryptids, including the elusive Cadborosaurus. While many enthusiasts are eager to accept eyewitness accounts and anecdotal evidence as valid proof of its existence, a critical examination of such claims is essential for a comprehensive understanding of the phenomenon. Eyewitness reports, while often compelling, can be influenced by various factors, including environmental conditions, emotional states, and cultural backgrounds. This skepticism is not meant to dismiss the experiences of witnesses but rather to contextualize them within a framework of scientific inquiry.

When reviewing Cadborosaurus sightings, it is important to consider the reliability of the sources. Many reports are anecdotal, relying on personal stories passed down through generations or shared in local communities. While these accounts can provide valuable insights into the lore surrounding Cadborosaurus, they must be scrutinized for consistency and accuracy. Discrepancies in descriptions, the influence of local myths, and the potential for misidentification of known marine animals all contribute to the complexity of validating such sightings. A rigorous approach to these accounts can help differentiate between genuine evidence and the embellishment of folklore.

Scientific studies and theories about Cadborosaurus often face similar challenges. Researchers must grapple with limited physical evidence, as the cryptid is primarily known through oral traditions and sporadic sightings. This scarcity of tangible data makes it difficult to apply conventional scientific methods. Many hypotheses about Cadborosaurus's existence stem from comparisons with known marine species and the possibility of undiscovered creatures in the ocean depths. However, these theories require careful examination and should be grounded in solid scientific principles rather than speculative narratives.

The portrayal of Cadborosaurus in popular culture and media also invites skepticism. Movies, documentaries, and artistic interpretations can sensationalize the myth, often prioritizing entertainment over factual accuracy. This can create a skewed perception of Cadborosaurus, leading to misconceptions about its characteristics and habitat. While creative depictions can inspire curiosity and interest in cryptozoology, they can also detract from serious discussions about the evidence and the importance of a methodical approach to inquiry.

Lastly, addressing the environmental impact on potential Cadborosaurus habitats is essential in the broader conversation about its existence. Changes in marine ecosystems due to climate change, pollution, and human activity may influence the populations of marine life that could be related to the

Cadborosaurus legend. Understanding these environmental factors can provide context for the cryptid's potential existence and its place within the coastal ecosystems. Engaging with these elements through a critical lens encourages a more nuanced appreciation of the search for Cadborosaurus, balancing enthusiasm with a commitment to evidence-based investigation.

CHAPTER 4

Cadborosaurus in Popular Culture

Representation in Literature

Representation in literature plays a crucial role in shaping the perception of cryptids, particularly in the case of Cadborosaurus, a legendary sea serpent said to inhabit the waters of the Pacific Northwest. This enigmatic creature has inspired a plethora of written works that range from academic studies to fictional narratives. These representations often reflect societal interests, fears, and curiosities surrounding the unknown. They serve as a medium through which enthusiasts can explore the rich tapestry of folklore, personal experiences, and scientific inquiry that envelops the mystery of Cadborosaurus.

Eyewitness accounts are a significant element in the literary representation of Cadborosaurus. Many narratives emerge from individuals who claim to have encountered the creature, often detailing their experiences with vivid descriptions and emotional weight. These personal testimonies contribute to a growing body of literature that underscores the importance of anecdotal evidence in the field of cryptozoology. As enthusiasts sift through these accounts, they encounter a spectrum of interpretations that range from skepticism to fervent belief, showcasing the diverse reactions people have to the prospect of an undiscovered marine species.

Scientific studies and theories also find their place in the literary representation of Cadborosaurus. Researchers delve into the biological plausibility of such a creature existing in modern times, drawing from marine biology, paleontology, and environmental science. Literature in this area often discusses the ecological aspects that could support the existence of Cadborosaurus, such as the rich biodiversity of the waters off the coast of British Columbia. This scientific lens adds credibility to the narrative, bridging the gap between folklore and empirical research, and inviting readers to consider the intersection of myth and reality.

The representation of Cadborosaurus extends beyond academic discourse into popular culture and media. Films, television shows, and literature have depicted Cadborosaurus, embedding it within a broader context of sea monsters and the allure of the unknown. These portrayals often reflect cultural anxieties and fascinations with the ocean as an unexplored frontier. Artistic interpretations and illustrations also amplify the mythical qualities of Cadborosaurus, allowing audiences to visualize the creature in ways that spark imagination and intrigue. This interplay between literature, art, and media not only captivates audiences but also fuels ongoing discussions about the creature's existence.

Lastly, historical accounts and folklore significantly enrich the literary narrative surrounding Cadborosaurus. Indigenous stories and local legends provide a foundation for understanding how this cryptid has been woven into the cultural fabric of coastal communities. These narratives often highlight humanity's longstanding relationship with the ocean, emphasizing themes of respect, fear, and reverence. As cryptozoology enthusiasts engage with these diverse representations, they not only deepen their understanding of Cadborosaurus but also appreciate the broader implications of how legends shape our perception of the natural world and our place within it.

Cadborosaurus in Film and Television

Cadborosaurus, a legendary sea serpent said to inhabit the coastal waters of the Pacific Northwest, has made a notable impact in film and television, capturing the imaginations of audiences and cryptozoology enthusiasts alike. Its appearances range from documentaries to fictional narratives, often blending folklore with imaginative storytelling. These portrayals not only highlight the creature's elusive nature but also emphasize the broader cultural fascination with cryptids. Through various media, Cadborosaurus serves as a symbol of mystery, inviting viewers to explore the thin line between myth and reality.

In documentaries, Cadborosaurus is frequently depicted alongside other cryptids, allowing viewers to engage with eyewitness accounts and scientific theories surrounding its existence. Programs dedicated to the exploration of unexplained phenomena often feature experts discussing the potential habitats and environmental conditions that could support such a creature. Eyewitness accounts are crucial in these films, as they provide personal narratives that validate the ongoing search for Cadborosaurus. The blending of expert opinions with compelling personal stories enhances the viewer's experience, fostering a deeper interest in the creature's legend.

Television shows that delve into the supernatural often include Cadborosaurus in their repertoire of mythical beings. These series frequently dramatize reports of sightings, using artistic interpretations to visualize encounters with the creature. The cinematic portrayal of Cadborosaurus varies widely, from terrifying sea monsters in horror-themed narratives to more whimsical representations in family-friendly programming. This diversity in representation reflects the creature's multifaceted nature, allowing it to resonate with different audience demographics while maintaining its status as an enigmatic entity.

Moreover, the influence of Cadborosaurus in popular culture extends beyond traditional media. It has inspired a range of artistic interpretations, from illustrations in books to themed merchandise. These creative expressions contribute to the ongoing dialogue about the creature, sparking curiosity and debate among enthusiasts. Artists often draw from historical accounts and folklore, incorporating elements that resonate with the mythos surrounding Cadborosaurus. This artistic engagement not only preserves the creature's legacy but also invites new generations to explore the narratives that have shaped its identity.

As the search for Cadborosaurus continues, its representation in film and television remains a powerful tool for education and exploration. Documentaries that focus on the environmental aspects of its habitat and the scientific investigations into its existence serve to legitimize the fascination with this cryptid. By weaving together narratives of folklore, scientific inquiry, and personal experiences, these media portrayals keep the legend of Cadborosaurus alive, encouraging ongoing discussions within the cryptozoological community and beyond.

Merchandise and Public Fascination

Merchandise related to Cadborosaurus has become a fascinating aspect of its cultural significance, appealing to cryptozoology enthusiasts and the general public alike. From plush toys to apparel featuring this elusive sea serpent, the market reflects a growing fascination with the creature. This merchandise not only serves as a way for fans to express their interest but also helps to perpetuate the lore surrounding Cadborosaurus. The proliferation of these products often draws attention to sightings and eyewitness accounts, further fueling curiosity and encouraging more individuals to explore the stories and scientific studies associated with this legendary creature.

Eyewitness accounts play a crucial role in the Cadborosaurus narrative, providing a foundation for the merchandise that often highlights these experiences. Many products depict specific sightings, capturing the essence of the moments that have sparked intrigue for generations. This connection between merchandise and real-life encounters emphasizes the importance of these stories, as they not only validate the existence of Cadborosaurus but also inspire artistic interpretations and illustrations that capture the imagination. As enthusiasts share their own experiences, the demand for related products continues to grow, creating a feedback loop that enriches the Cadborosaurus narrative.

Scientific studies and theories surrounding Cadborosaurus also influence the types of merchandise available. Items often incorporate elements from these studies, such as diagrams that depict the creature's anatomy or hypothetical habitats. This intersection of science and folklore encourages a deeper understanding of the potential realities of Cadborosaurus, enticing buyers who seek not just novelty but also a connection to the speculative research that surrounds this cryptid. As the academic community continues to explore the possibilities of its existence, merchandise serves as a tangible link to ongoing investigations and discussions.

In popular culture and media, Cadborosaurus has captured the attention of filmmakers and artists alike, leading to a variety of documentaries and creative expressions that further amplify its presence. Merchandise often reflects this cultural portrayal, with designs inspired by documentary filmmaking and artistic interpretations seen in films and TV shows. These products help to solidify Cadborosaurus's place in contemporary mythology, allowing enthusiasts to carry a piece of this fascination into their daily lives. As more films explore the cryptid's mysteries, merchandise becomes a way for fans to engage with the narratives presented on screen.

The environmental impact on Cadborosaurus habitats also plays a role in shaping merchandise discourse. As awareness of ecological issues increases, products that promote conservation efforts or educate consumers about the potential habitats of Cadborosaurus are gaining traction. Such items resonate with a community that values both the search for cryptids and the preservation of the ecosystems they inhabit. This blend of environmental consciousness and cryptid enthusiasm highlights the importance of responsible merchandise practices, ensuring that the allure of Cadborosaurus continues to inspire future generations while advocating for the protection of its natural environment.

CHAPTER 5

Cryptozoology and the Hunt

The Role of Cryptozoologists

The role of cryptozoologists in the ongoing investigation of Cadborosaurus is multifaceted, involving both scientific inquiry and community engagement. These dedicated researchers seek to uncover the truth behind reports of this elusive sea creature, often described as a large serpent or dragon-like being inhabiting the coastal waters of British Columbia. By examining eyewitness accounts and historical sightings, cryptozoologists work to distinguish between genuine evidence and myth, fostering a deeper understanding of the cultural significance of Cadborosaurus in maritime folklore.

In their pursuit to validate the existence of Cadborosaurus, cryptozoologists employ a variety of scientific methods. Field studies are crucial, as researchers often embark on expeditions to areas known for reported sightings. These trips may include the use of sonar technology, underwater cameras, and even drones to capture potential evidence of the creature. By documenting the environmental conditions and habitats where sightings occur, cryptozoologists contribute to a growing body of knowledge that may eventually lead to the discovery of new species or a better understanding of the ecosystem in which these elusive beings might reside.

Eyewitness accounts serve as both a valuable resource and a challenge for cryptozoologists. While personal testimonies can provide insight into the creature's characteristics and behavior, they are also subject to scrutiny due to the potential for misidentification or exaggeration. Cryptozoologists meticulously analyze these reports, often comparing them with similar sightings of other sea monsters, to discern patterns and establish credibility. This rigorous evaluation helps to build a more reliable narrative surrounding Cadborosaurus, bridging the gap between folklore and scientific inquiry.

The impact of Cadborosaurus on popular culture and media cannot be understated, as it has inspired numerous artistic interpretations, documentaries, and fictional portrayals. Cryptozoologists often collaborate with filmmakers and artists to create compelling narratives that captivate audiences while remaining rooted in the quest for truth. By engaging with the public through various media, these researchers aim to raise awareness about the importance of marine conservation and the preservation of habitats that may support unknown species, including Cadborosaurus.

Ultimately, the role of cryptozoologists in the search for Cadborosaurus extends beyond mere investigation; it encompasses the promotion of environmental stewardship and the appreciation of biodiversity. As they navigate the complex interplay between science and folklore, these researchers foster a community of enthusiasts who share a passion for uncovering the mysteries of our natural world. The ongoing exploration of Cadborosaurus not only enriches our understanding of cryptids but also underscores the importance of protecting the environments that give rise to such legends.

Methodologies for Searching

Methodologies for searching for Cadborosaurus encompass a wide array of approaches that combine scientific rigor with the adventurous spirit inherent to cryptozoology. Researchers and enthusiasts alike utilize a blend of traditional field-work, modern technology, and historical analysis to gather evidence and pursue sightings of this elusive sea creature. By understanding and employing varied methodologies, cryptozoologists can enhance their search efforts, drawing upon diverse resources and perspectives.

One primary methodology involves the meticulous documentation of eyewitness accounts and sightings. Engaging with local communities along the coast, researchers often conduct interviews with individuals who claim to have encountered

Cadborosaurus. Compiling these accounts into a comprehensive database allows for the identification of patterns and common characteristics associated with sightings. This qualitative data serves as a foundational element for further investigation, helping to establish credibility and pinpoint potential hotspots for future searches.

In addition to gathering anecdotal evidence, scientific studies play a crucial role in the search for Cadborosaurus. Researchers employ techniques such as environmental DNA sampling to analyze water samples for genetic material that could confirm the creature's existence. This method provides a non-invasive means of exploration, allowing scientists to assess the biodiversity of coastal ecosystems and identify any unusual or unknown species that may contribute to the Cadborosaurus legend. Coupled with oceanographic studies that examine habitat conditions, these scientific approaches help to create a clearer picture of where Cadborosaurus might thrive.

Technological advancements have also transformed the methodologies used in the search for Cadborosaurus. Drones equipped with high-resolution cameras can provide aerial views of coastal areas, enabling researchers to cover vast stretches of shoreline and observe hard-to-reach locations. Underwater drones and remote-operated vehicles equipped with cameras and sensors can explore depths that human divers cannot access, offering a new frontier in the search for elusive marine creatures. The integration of these technologies allows for a more efficient and comprehensive approach to gathering evidence and conducting fieldwork.

Lastly, the influence of popular culture and media cannot be overlooked in the methodologies for searching. Documentaries, podcasts, and social media platforms serve as valuable tools for raising awareness and sharing findings related to Cadborosaurus. These mediums can inspire public interest and encourage amateur enthusiasts to contribute their own sightings and research. By fostering a collaborative environment, the search for Cadborosaurus becomes a collective effort, uniting both seasoned cryptozoologists and curious newcomers in the quest to uncover the truth behind this legendary creature.

Case Studies of Failed and Successful Expeditions

The exploration of Cadborosaurus, a creature steeped in folklore and mystery, has seen both triumphs and pitfalls throughout its history. Successful expeditions often combine thorough research, community engagement, and an understanding of local ecosystems. One notable example is the 1930 expedition led by naturalist Dr. J. B. H. Smith, who meticulously documented eyewitness accounts and gathered photographs claiming to depict the creature. His approach not only provided significant insights into the habitats where sightings occurred but also fostered a sense of credibility among skeptics. The combination of scientific inquiry and local folklore helped cement Cadborosaurus in the public consciousness, leading to increased interest and further investigations.

In contrast, there have been expeditions that failed to yield tangible evidence or meaningful findings. A well-documented case is the 2009 attempt by a team of marine biologists and cryptozoologists who sought to capture sonar images of Cadborosaurus. Despite employing advanced technology and thorough planning, the expedition faced numerous challenges, including equipment malfunctions and inclement weather. The lack of credible sightings during their expedition led to skepticism about the validity of the creature's existence, illustrating how inadequate preparation and reliance on technology without a grounding in local knowledge can hinder success.

Eyewitness accounts play a critical role in the ongoing search for Cadborosaurus, and studies of these claims often reveal intriguing patterns. For instance, a series of sightings reported in the 1980s off the coast of British Columbia highlighted similarities in descriptions among different witnesses. These included characteristics such as the creature's elongated body, humped back, and serpentine movements. Successful expeditions have leveraged these collective narratives to target specific locales believed to be frequented by the cryptid. This highlights the importance of community involvement and the validation of personal experiences to inspire further investigation.

The impact of popular culture on the perception of Cadborosaurus cannot be understated. Documentaries and television shows often sensationalize the search for cryptids, which can lead to misinterpretations of scientific findings and eye-witness accounts. However, successful media portrayals have also sparked genuine interest, encouraging viewers to explore the historical and ecological context surrounding the creature. The balance lies in presenting factual information while engaging audiences through storytelling, as seen in documentaries that feature interviews with local fishermen and historians, weaving together folklore and scientific inquiry.

Environmental factors significantly influence the habitats of potential Cadborosaurus sightings. Successful expeditions have often coincided with periods of environmental awareness, emphasizing the need to protect marine ecosystems. Studies have shown that changes in water temperature, pollution, and overfishing can impact the availability of prey for large marine creatures. Understanding these ecological dynamics not only aids in the search for Cadborosaurus but also highlights the importance of conservation efforts in maintaining the delicate balance of coastal ecosystems. By integrating scientific research, community narratives, and environmental considerations, expeditions can create a comprehensive framework for exploring the mysteries of Cadborosaurus and its place in the natural world.

CHAPTER 6

Historical Accounts and Folklore

Indigenous Stories and Legends

Indigenous cultures along the Pacific Coast have long held rich traditions of storytelling, with many tales featuring mysterious creatures that echo the characteristics of Cadborosaurus. These narratives often serve not only as entertainment but also as means to convey lessons, cultural values, and explanations for the natural world. By examining these indigenous stories, we can gain insights into how early peoples perceived the ocean and its inhabitants, including the potential existence of creatures that resemble Cadborosaurus. These legends are critical in understanding the local ecological and spiritual landscapes that shaped their societies.

One prominent figure in these narratives is the "Naitaka," often described as a sea serpent or monster that inhabits the waters off the coast of British Columbia. The Naitaka is portrayed as a powerful and respected being, capable of both harm and protection, depending on the nature of human interactions with the environment. This duality reflects a deep understanding of the ocean's unpredictable nature and emphasizes the importance of coexistence and respect for all creatures. Such stories may have inspired contemporary accounts of Cadborosaurus, as they highlight the potential for large, enigmatic beings lurking beneath the waves.

Eyewitness accounts of Cadborosaurus often draw parallels to these indigenous legends, with many sightings reporting a creature resembling the descriptions of the Naitaka. These contemporary encounters frequently occur in the same areas where indigenous stories have been told for generations, suggesting a cultural continuity that links past beliefs with modern cryptozoological pursuits. This connection raises intriguing questions about the persistence of these myths and their potential basis in real encounters with unknown marine life.

Scientific studies and theories about Cadborosaurus also benefit from the narratives handed down through generations. Researchers often look to folklore for clues that may inform their investigations, as these stories can provide historical context and anecdotal evidence regarding the creature's habitat and behavior. By considering the ecological conditions and marine biodiversity described in indigenous legends, scientists can formulate hypotheses that guide their search for Cadborosaurus in today's waters. Furthermore, these narratives challenge the scientific community to maintain an open mind regarding the existence of cryptids and the interplay between culture and natural history.

The cultural significance of Cadborosaurus extends into popular culture and media, where artistic interpretations and documentaries often draw inspiration from indigenous stories and legends. These representations not only keep the legend alive but also spark interest in cryptozoology among broader audiences. By weaving indigenous narratives into the fabric of modern storytelling, filmmakers and artists contribute to a growing fascination with the unknown, encouraging viewers to explore the depths of the ocean and the mysteries it holds. This blend of folklore and contemporary exploration underscores the enduring legacy of indigenous stories in the ongoing search for Cadborosaurus and similar creatures of the deep.

19th Century Sightings and Reports

The 19th century marked a pivotal era for the legend of Cadborosaurus, as a series of sightings and reports began to capture public interest and fuel speculation about this elusive creature. The coastal waters of British Columbia became the backdrop for numerous encounters, with eyewitness accounts often describing a long, serpentine creature resembling a sea serpent. These reports varied in detail, yet many shared common characteristics, such as a large, undulating body and a head that resembled that of a horse or a seal. Such descriptions not only contributed to the growing mythos surrounding Cadborosaurus but also inspired a sense of wonder and intrigue that would resonate through the following decades.

Among the most notable sightings of the 19th century was an incident in 1892, when a group of fishermen off the coast of Cadboro Bay reported seeing a large creature breach the surface of the water. They described it as having a lengthy neck and a smooth, grayish skin, drawing parallels to the infamous Loch Ness Monster. This sighting was instrumental in solidifying Cadborosaurus's place in maritime folklore, as local newspapers picked up the story, further spreading tales of the beast's existence. Eyewitness accounts such as this not only captivated the public's imagination but also prompted early investigations into the phenomenon by both amateur enthusiasts and serious researchers.

Scientific interest in Cadborosaurus grew during the latter part of the century, with various theories attempting to explain the creature's origins. Some researchers speculated that these sightings could be attributed to misidentified marine animals, such as basking sharks or seals, which, when seen at a distance or in poor visibility, could appear to fit the descriptions of Cadborosaurus. Others posited that the creature might be a remnant of prehistoric marine reptiles, awakening interest in paleontological studies. This intersection of cryptozoology and scientific inquiry laid the groundwork for future investigations, as both skeptics and believers sought to unravel the mystery of the creature.

As the 19th century progressed, the allure of Cadborosaurus permeated popular culture, leading to artistic interpretations and illustrations that further shaped public perception. Artists began to depict the creature in various forms, often blending elements of known marine life with imaginative features. These representations not only served to entertain but also contributed to the mythos surrounding Cadborosaurus, embedding it deeper into the cultural consciousness of coastal communities. The blend of fact and fiction in these artistic renderings fueled both folklore and the burgeoning field of cryptozoology, creating a rich tapestry of stories and images that would be referenced for generations.

The environmental context of the 19th century also played a crucial role in shaping the narrative of Cadborosaurus. Rapid industrialization and increased maritime activity altered coastal ecosystems, potentially affecting the habitats of marine life in the region. This environmental impact may have contributed to the frequency of sightings, as changes in prey availability and water quality could have drawn previously hidden creatures closer to the shore. The interplay between the natural world and human activity not only provides a backdrop for the sightings of Cadborosaurus but also invites further exploration into how our understanding of marine ecosystems can influence the search for cryptids like this enigmatic sea serpent.

Modern Folklore and Its Evolution

Modern folklore surrounding Cadborosaurus exemplifies the dynamic interplay between myth and contemporary culture. This elusive sea serpent, reputedly inhabiting the waters off the coast of British Columbia, has transcended its origins in local legend to become a subject of intrigue among cryptozoology enthusiasts. Eyewitness accounts, ranging from fishermen to casual beachgoers, have contributed to a growing narrative that blends anecdotal evidence with the thrill of the unknown. These stories often reflect societal values and fears, echoing the deep-rooted human fascination with the mysterious and the monstrous.

As the digital age has accelerated the spread of information, sightings and claims regarding Cadborosaurus have proliferated online. Social media platforms and forums dedicated to cryptozoology serve as modern campfires, where individuals recount their encounters and share illustrations and photographs. This shift not only fuels public interest but also encourages a more communal effort in the search for evidence. The evolution of this folklore can be traced through the lenses of scientific inquiry and popular culture, both of which shape and are shaped by these narratives.

Scientific studies on Cadborosaurus often grapple with the challenge of validating anecdotal evidence while navigating the skepticism that surrounds cryptid research. Researchers seek to balance rigorous scientific methods with the need to understand the cultural significance of these stories. Theories about the creature's existence range from the identification of known marine species to more speculative hypotheses involving unknown organisms. Engaging with these theories allows for a richer dialogue between folklore and science, highlighting the importance of interdisciplinary approaches in understanding the Cadborosaurus phenomenon.

In popular culture, Cadborosaurus has inspired numerous artistic interpretations, from illustrations to documentaries. This representation in various media not only cements its place in the collective imagination but also raises questions about the nature of belief and artistic license. Documentaries that focus on the hunt for Cadborosaurus often blend investigative journalism with storytelling, captivating audiences while attempting to shed light on the enigma surrounding this legendary creature. Such portrayals can influence public perception, often straddling the line between skepticism and belief.

The environmental context in which Cadborosaurus is said to exist adds another layer to its folklore. Changes in marine ecosystems due to climate change, pollution, and human activity may impact the habitats that sustain cryptids like Cadborosaurus. Understanding these environmental factors is crucial not only for cryptozoologists but also for conservationists who recognize the interconnectedness of folklore and ecological health. As modern folklore continues to evolve, the narrative of Cadborosaurus serves as a poignant reminder of humanity's enduring fascination with the unknown and the stories that arise from it.

CHAPTER 7

Comparisons with Other Sea Monsters

Similarities to Nessie and Other Lake Monsters

The fascination with Cadborosaurus is often paralleled with the enduring legends of other lake monsters, particularly the infamous Loch Ness Monster, affectionately known as Nessie. Both creatures share a common narrative thread woven through the folklore of their respective regions, captivating the imaginations of cryptozoologists and casual observers alike. Sightings of Cadborosaurus, much like those of Nessie, frequently describe a long, serpentine body and an elusive nature that seems to defy scientific explanation. The similarities in their physical descriptions have led to intriguing discussions about the existence and characteristics of such cryptids, especially given the geographical and ecological contexts in which they are said to inhabit.

Eyewitness accounts from both Cadborosaurus and Nessie enthusiasts reveal a striking resemblance in the reported behavior of these creatures. Witnesses often describe them as exhibiting a blend of grace and power when navigating their watery domains. Whether it is the way Cadborosaurus reportedly undulates through the waters of the Pacific Northwest or the manner in which Nessie is said to glide through Loch Ness, the commonalities in their movements foster a sense of shared identity among lake monsters. This has prompted some researchers to explore the possibility of a single species or a similar lineage that could explain the prevalence of such sightings across different bodies of water.

The scientific studies surrounding both Cadborosaurus and Nessie often engage in the contentious debate between folklore and empirical evidence. While many argue that the lack of physical evidence for either creature undermines their existence, proponents of cryptozoology point to the rich historical accounts and anecdotal evidence that continue to surface. The stories of Cadborosaurus, much like those of Nessie, are deeply embedded in the cultural fabric of their respective regions, suggesting that these legends serve a purpose beyond mere entertainment. The ongoing search for both creatures has inspired scientific inquiries that seek to bridge the gap between myth and reality, examining the ecological conditions that might support such beings.

In popular culture, Cadborosaurus and Nessie have become iconic symbols of the cryptid phenomenon, inspiring a multitude of artistic interpretations and media portrayals. From documentaries to children's books, the allure of these creatures has permeated various forms of storytelling, often highlighting their mysterious natures. This shared cultural significance has fostered a sense of community among cryptozoology enthusiasts who are drawn to the thrill of the hunt and the potential discovery of something extraordinary. By examining the narratives surrounding both Cadborosaurus and Nessie, one can appreciate how these legends have evolved and continue to inspire curiosity and exploration.

The environmental impact on the habitats of both Cadborosaurus and Nessie has become a focal point for understanding their potential existence. Changes in water quality, climate, and human activity in areas like the Pacific Northwest and the Scottish Highlands can significantly affect the ecosystems that purportedly support these cryptids. As researchers delve into the environmental factors that could sustain such elusive species, the parallels between Cadborosaurus and Nessie become not only a matter of folklore but also a pressing ecological concern. The continued interest in these lake monsters serves as a reminder of the delicate balance between myth, science, and the natural world, urging us to consider the implications of our interactions with these mysterious habitats.

Theories Linking Cadborosaurus to Ancient Myths
The connection between Cadborosaurus and ancient myths is a fascinating aspect of cryptozoology that invites deeper exploration. Throughout history, many cultures along the Pacific coast have shared stories of sea monsters that eerily resemble Cadborosaurus. From the indigenous legends of the Salish Sea to the tales passed down through generations by coastal communities, these narratives often describe large, serpentine creatures with similar characteristics to those attributed to Cadborosaurus. The alignment of these ancient mythological accounts with modern sightings provides compelling evidence that this cryptid may not just be a product of contemporary imagination but rather a continuation of a long-standing mythological tradition.

One prominent theory suggests that Cadborosaurus may have served as a cultural touchstone for coastal peoples, embodying their fears and respect for the ocean. The creature often represents the unknown, a symbol of nature's untamed power. In this context, Cadborosaurus could be viewed as a manifestation of the human experience with the sea, reflecting both the dangers and the mysteries that it holds. Such interpretations offer insight into how ancient societies understood their environment and the creatures within it, potentially influencing contemporary sightings and encounters.

Moreover, the rich tapestry of folklore surrounding Cadborosaurus includes various accounts that describe similar entities across different cultures. For instance, the mythical sea monsters of Norse mythology and the legendary Kraken share traits with Cadborosaurus, suggesting that these stories may derive from common sea serpent archetypes. This cross-cultural comparison not only highlights the universality of the sea monster motif but also raises questions about the origins of these legends. Were they inspired by actual encounters with large marine animals, or do they emerge solely from cultural imaginations? The parallels between these tales and modern-day sightings of Cadborosaurus encourage further investigation into the historical context of these myths.

Scientific studies have also sought to understand the potential links between Cadborosaurus and ancient myths. Researchers often examine the biological and ecological aspects of the creature and its potential habitats, considering how these might intersect with the narratives held by local populations. By analyzing eyewitness accounts and comparing them to historical descriptions, scientists can develop hypotheses about the creature's existence and its role within the marine ecosystem. Such studies not only enrich our understanding of Cadborosaurus but also provide a scientific lens through which to view the myths that have surrounded it for centuries.

In popular culture, Cadborosaurus has found a place alongside other legendary sea monsters, inspiring artistic interpretations and media portrayals that further cement its mythic status. Documentaries and films exploring the cryptid have often referenced historical accounts and folklore, demonstrating how these stories shape public perception and interest in the creature. As audiences engage with these narratives, they contribute to the ongoing mythology of Cadborosaurus, perpetuating the cycle of myth and reality. This interplay between ancient myths and modern fascination underscores the enduring legacy of Cadborosaurus as a symbol of the mysteries lurking beneath the waves, inviting continued exploration and discovery within the field of cryptozoology.

Divergent Characteristics

Cadborosaurus, often described as a long, serpentine creature, exhibits a variety of characteristics that set it apart from other cryptids and sea monsters in folklore. Eyewitness accounts frequently depict this creature with a horse-like head, elongated body, and prominent humps, reminiscent of a marine dinosaur. These physical traits have led to a range of interpretations in both artistic representations and scientific analyses. The diversity in descriptions may stem from the varying environments where sightings occur, suggesting that Cadborosaurus may adapt its appearance based on habitat, prey availability, and other ecological factors.

In the realm of cryptozoology, Cadborosaurus stands out not just for its unique morphology but also for the rich tapestry of historical accounts that surround it. Native American folklore has long included tales of a sea serpent inhabiting the coastal waters of British Columbia, which connects the modern sightings to ancient narratives. This continuity of stories enhances the creature's legitimacy in the eyes of enthusiasts and researchers alike. Furthermore, the blend of history and eyewitness reports creates a multifaceted picture of Cadborosaurus that continues to intrigue those who study cryptids and their cultural significance.

Scientific studies regarding Cadborosaurus often grapple with the challenge of a lack of concrete evidence. While some researchers propose that the creature could be a misidentified species, such as a large marine mammal or even a basking shark, others consider the possibility of an undiscovered species entirely. This debate highlights the divergent characteristics of Cadborosaurus, suggesting that it may not fit neatly into existing classifications of marine life. The ongoing search for scientific validation also emphasizes the importance of rigorous methodologies in cryptozoological research, as enthusiasts strive to bridge the gap between folklore and empirical evidence.

Cadborosaurus has made a significant impact on popular culture and media, influencing everything from documentary filmmaking to artistic interpretations. Its enigmatic nature has led to numerous films, books, and television shows that explore the legend of this sea serpent. These portrayals often amplify the creature's mystical qualities, contributing to a broader cultural fascination with cryptids. As artists and filmmakers depict Cadborosaurus in various styles, they reflect both the creature's legendary status and the allure of the unknown, capturing the imagination of audiences worldwide.

The environmental context of Cadborosaurus habitats also plays a critical role in understanding its characteristics. Coastal ecosystems, such as kelp forests and deep-sea trenches, provide a rich tapestry of biodiversity that could support such a creature. Changes in these environments, driven by human activity and climate change, may influence sightings and behavior. As cryptozoologists continue their hunt for Cadborosaurus, it becomes increasingly important to consider how ecological shifts affect the existence and visibility of this elusive cryptid, emphasizing the need for a holistic approach in both research and conservation efforts.

CHAPTER 8

Artistic Interpretations and Illustrations

Historical Artwork Depicting Cadborosaurus

Throughout history, the mysterious Cadborosaurus has captured the imagination of artists, leading to a variety of historical artworks that depict this enigmatic sea creature. These artistic interpretations often reflect the cultural context and maritime folklore of the regions where sightings have occurred, particularly along the Pacific Northwest coast. Many of these artworks served not only as illustrations of the creature but also as a means to convey the local lore associated with it, fostering a deeper connection between communities and their maritime environment.

One of the earliest known depictions of Cadborosaurus can be traced back to Indigenous peoples of the Pacific Northwest, who often included serpentine creatures in their art and storytelling. These representations often symbolized the power and mystery of the ocean, reflecting a reverence for the natural world and its hidden wonders. The stories surrounding these images spoke of encounters with the creature, imbuing it with a sense of both fear and fascination that resonates with contemporary cryptozoological interests.

As European settlers arrived in the region, they brought with them their own interpretations of local legends, including those of Cadborosaurus. Artists began to create renderings that merged Indigenous imagery with European artistic styles, often depicting the creature in a more monstrous light. These artworks played a significant role in shaping public perception, contributing to the mythos surrounding Cadborosaurus as a fearsome sea serpent that lurked in the depths, waiting to emerge in moments of coastal peril.

In the 20th century, as interest in cryptids surged, artists began to produce more scientifically-minded interpretations of Cadborosaurus, drawing on eyewitness accounts and scientific studies to inform their work. These depictions often sought to balance the fantastical elements of the creature with a semblance of realism, incorporating anatomical features hypothesized from reports of sightings. This blending of folklore and science allowed for a renewed dialogue between the realms of art and cryptozoology, inviting enthusiasts to consider the possibilities of what lies beneath the waves.

Today, contemporary artists continue to explore the theme of Cadborosaurus through various mediums, from paintings to digital illustrations. These modern interpretations not only honor historical depictions but also reflect current understanding and theories about the creature's existence. As the quest for Cadborosaurus persists, the artwork surrounding it remains a vital aspect of its cultural narrative, inspiring new generations of cryptozoology enthusiasts to engage with the mysteries of the deep and the stories that continue to evolve around this elusive marine cryptid.

Modern Artistic Representations

Modern artistic representations of Cadborosaurus play a significant role in shaping public perception and understanding of this elusive cryptid. Artists and illustrators have taken on the challenge of visualizing a creature that remains largely shrouded in mystery, often drawing from eyewitness accounts and historical descriptions. These representations range from realistic interpretations that attempt to capture the essence of a large marine serpent to more fantastical depictions that emphasize the creature's mythical qualities. Each artistic portrayal provides a unique lens through which enthusiasts can engage with the lore surrounding Cadborosaurus.

Illustrators often rely on a combination of scientific knowledge and imaginative speculation when depicting Cadborosaurus. Many of these artists study marine biology and the anatomy of known sea creatures to create a plausible representation. For instance, some renderings showcase features similar to those of known marine animals, such as elongated bodies, flippers, and serpentine tails, which align with descriptions from eyewitness accounts. This blending of fact and fiction not only enriches the visual narrative but also supports the ongoing discussions within the cryptozoological community regarding the creature's potential existence.

In popular culture, Cadborosaurus has inspired various forms of artistic interpretation, including paintings, digital art, and even sculptures. These artworks often reflect the cultural context in which they were created, revealing societal attitudes towards cryptids and the natural world. Documentaries and films have also incorporated artistic elements to dramatize sightings and encounters, enhancing the storytelling aspect of Cadborosaurus lore. By using imagery that evokes curiosity and wonder, these creative expressions contribute to the enduring fascination with the creature and its possible habitats.

The evolution of artistic representations of Cadborosaurus can also be tied to advancements in technology. Digital art tools have allowed artists to experiment with textures, colors, and lighting, resulting in more dynamic and immersive illustrations. Artists can now create lifelike animations that depict hypothetical encounters with Cadborosaurus in a way that was not possible with traditional media. These modern techniques have broadened the reach of Cadborosaurus-related art, making it accessible to a wider audience and fostering community engagement among cryptozoology enthusiasts.

Furthermore, the environmental context of Cadborosaurus habitats has become a focal point for many contemporary artists. As concerns about climate change and habitat degradation grow, some artworks reflect these challenges, portraying Cadborosaurus within ecosystems that are under threat. This artistic approach not only serves to highlight the importance of conservation but also invites viewers to consider the implications of human activity on the legendary creature's existence. In this way, modern artistic representations of

Cadborosaurus do more than just visualize a cryptid; they inspire dialogue about the intersection of myth, science, and environmental stewardship.

The Influence of Art on Public Perception

Art has long served as a powerful medium for shaping public perception, particularly in the realm of cryptozoology. The enigmatic nature of creatures like Cadborosaurus, a legendary sea serpent rumored to inhabit the waters off the coast of British Columbia, has inspired countless artistic interpretations. These representations range from illustrations in books and magazines to sculptures and digital art. Each piece contributes to the narrative surrounding Cadborosaurus, influencing how the public perceives its existence and the mystery of the unknown.

Illustrations of Cadborosaurus often draw on the eyewitness accounts and historical descriptions of the creature, blending elements of realism with the fantastical. Artists take creative liberties to portray what they believe the creature might look like, often emphasizing its serpentine form and the dramatic settings of coastal waters. These artistic renditions can evoke wonder and curiosity, encouraging audiences to engage with the concept of sea monsters more openly. The visual allure of these representations can lead to increased interest in cryptozoology, inviting individuals to explore the lore and science behind such creatures.

In addition to traditional art forms, the influence of popular media cannot be overlooked. Documentaries, films, and television series have also played a crucial role in shaping perceptions of Cadborosaurus. These productions often dramatize sightings and historical accounts, bringing the creature to life in ways that captivate audiences. The blending of fiction and reality in such media can lead to a phenomenon known as the "media effect," where viewers may become more inclined to believe in the existence of Cadborosaurus after being exposed to these compelling narratives.

Moreover, the intersection of art and scientific inquiry is significant in the ongoing search for Cadborosaurus. Many cryptozoologists rely on visual art to complement their research, using illustrations to depict potential habitats and behaviors of the creature. This collaboration between artists and scientists fosters a greater understanding of the ecological context in which Cadborosaurus might exist. It encourages a multidisciplinary approach, blending creativity with empirical study, which can enhance public interest and engagement in cryptozoological research.

Ultimately, the influence of art on public perception extends beyond mere aesthetics; it shapes the narrative surrounding Cadborosaurus and fuels the passion of cryptozoology enthusiasts. The interplay between artistic expression and cryptid lore invites a broader audience to explore the mysteries of the sea, fostering a sense of wonder and curiosity. As perceptions evolve through artistic and media portrayals, they contribute to the ongoing dialogue about the relationship between humanity and the unknown, prompting us to reconsider what lies beneath the waves.

CHAPTER 9

Environmental Impact on Cadborosaurus Habitats

Climate Change and Its Effects

Climate change poses significant threats to marine ecosystems, affecting not only well-documented species but also cryptids like Cadborosaurus. The gradual rise in ocean temperatures, coupled with increased acidification due to higher carbon dioxide levels, alters the delicate balance of marine habitats. These changes can disrupt the food chain, impacting prey availability for elusive creatures like Cadborosaurus, which is rumored to inhabit the coastal waters of the Pacific Northwest. As cryptozoologists seek evidence of its existence, understanding the environmental shifts is crucial for understanding where and how Cadborosaurus might survive.

Coastal regions, often considered the primary habitat for Cadborosaurus sightings, are experiencing significant changes due to climate change. Rising sea levels threaten to inundate critical areas where these creatures may reside. Increased storm intensity and frequency can further erode shorelines and disrupt ecosystems, potentially driving cryptids further offshore or into less accessible waters. These environmental transformations not only challenge the survival of known marine species but may also hinder the chances of encountering Cadborosaurus, as potential sightings become rarer in increasingly altered landscapes.

The impact of climate change extends beyond habitat loss; it also affects the distribution and behavior of marine life. As ocean temperatures rise, species typically found in specific regions may migrate to cooler waters, potentially altering the ecological dynamics of those areas. This shift raises questions about the relationship between Cadborosaurus and its prey. If traditional food sources become scarce or migrate, this may push Cadborosaurus to adapt in ways that could influence its sightings and interactions with humans. Cryptozoologists must consider these factors when analyzing eyewitness accounts and historical folklore, as changes in marine life behavior could correlate with altered reports of Cadborosaurus encounters.

Scientific studies exploring the relationship between climate change and marine ecosystems provide valuable insights for cryptozoologists investigating Cadborosaurus. Researchers have documented the effects of warming waters on marine biodiversity, which can serve as a backdrop for understanding the potential challenges faced by cryptids. By examining shifts in fish populations and the health of coastal environments, enthusiasts can form hypotheses about how Cadborosaurus may respond to these threats. This scientific approach also reinforces the importance of interdisciplinary research in cryptozoology, bridging folklore and contemporary ecological studies to create a more comprehensive understanding of this enigmatic creature.

As Cadborosaurus remains a steadfast figure in popular culture and media, the narrative surrounding its existence is increasingly intertwined with environmental issues. Documentaries and artistic interpretations often reflect the urgency of preserving coastal ecosystems, which are critical not just for known species but also for the survival of cryptids. Highlighting these connections can inspire a broader audience to appreciate the importance of conservation efforts, ensuring that the search for Cadborosaurus and the protection of its habitat remain relevant and urgent. In doing so, cryptozoologists can advocate for a future where both the myth and reality of Cadborosaurus co-exist harmoniously within a healthier marine environment.

Human Activity and Habitat Destruction

Human activity has profoundly impacted marine ecosystems, leading to habitat destruction that poses significant threats to the survival of elusive creatures like Cadborosaurus. Coastal development, pollution, and overfishing have altered the habitats where these cryptids are believed to thrive. As urban areas expand, natural shorelines are replaced with concrete structures, disrupting the delicate balance of coastal ecosystems. This transformation not only affects the local flora and fauna but also diminishes the chances of Cadborosaurus sightings, as their preferred habitats become fragmented or entirely lost.

Pollution, particularly from industrial runoff and plastic waste, further exacerbates the degradation of marine environments. Contaminants can accumulate in the food chain, impacting the health of marine species that Cadborosaurus may rely on for sustenance. The decline of prey species due to pollution can lead to a scarcity of food, making it difficult for these cryptids to thrive. Additionally, the presence of pollutants can create an inhospitable environment for Cadborosaurus and other marine life, potentially driving them away from areas where they were once commonly sighted.

Overfishing presents another significant challenge to the ecosystems that support Cadborosaurus populations. As fish stocks dwindle, the natural balance of the marine food web is disrupted. This not only affects the availability of prey for Cadborosaurus but also alters the overall biodiversity of coastal waters. The removal of key species can lead to an ecological imbalance, further threatening the survival of both known and unknown marine creatures. Cryptozoologists and enthusiasts alike must consider how these changes in fish populations could influence the behavior and distribution of Cadborosaurus.

The cultural significance of creatures like Cadborosaurus has often been tied to their habitats, with many historical accounts and folklore reflecting the relationship between local communities and their coastal environments. As habitat destruction continues, the stories and sightings that have captivated cryptozoology enthusiasts may become less frequent. The loss of these narratives diminishes our understanding of Cadborosaurus and its place within the natural world, highlighting the importance of preserving not just the physical environment but also the cultural lore that surrounds it.

Efforts to document and study Cadborosaurus are increasingly intertwined with environmental conservation initiatives. As awareness grows regarding the impacts of human activity on marine habitats, there is a push to balance the pursuit of cryptozoological research with the need for sustainable practices. Documentaries and media focused on Cadborosaurus often emphasize the importance of protecting coastal ecosystems, reinforcing the idea that the future of these cryptids may depend on our collective responsibility to safeguard their habitats. In this way, the hunt for Cadborosaurus becomes more than just a quest for a legendary creature; it transforms into a vital endeavor for environmental stewardship and the preservation of our planet's rich biodiversity.

Conservation Efforts and Their Importance

Conservation efforts aimed at protecting the habitats of elusive creatures like Cadborosaurus are crucial for both the preservation of biodiversity and the potential discovery of new species. The coastal regions where Cadborosaurus is believed to reside are often vulnerable to pollution, climate change, and industrial activities. By promoting sustainable practices and safeguarding marine ecosystems, conservationists aim to create an environment where cryptids like Cadborosaurus can thrive, thus also benefiting the myriad of known species that share these habitats. This effort not only supports potential sightings and research but is also vital in maintaining the delicate balance of coastal ecosystems that sustain numerous marine life forms.

The importance of public awareness and education in conservation cannot be overstated. Engaging the community through workshops, informative campaigns, and citizen science projects can foster a deeper understanding of the ecological significance of coastal environments. By raising awareness about Cadborosaurus and its potential existence, enthusiasts can inspire more people to appreciate and protect the natural world. This grassroots involvement is essential for mobilizing support for conservation initiatives and can lead to increased funding and resources for research and habitat protection efforts.

Scientific studies focusing on environmental impacts provide valuable insights into how human activities affect the habitats of potential cryptids. Research on water quality, temperature fluctuations, and food chain dynamics helps in constructing a clearer picture of the challenges these creatures may face. Understanding these factors is not only crucial for the survival of Cadborosaurus but also enhances the overall knowledge of marine biology. By addressing these scientific questions, researchers can better advocate for specific conservation measures aimed at mitigating adverse environmental impacts that threaten both known and unknown species.

Historically, the folklore surrounding Cadborosaurus has emphasized its mysterious nature, often attributing sightings to the uncanny and the unknown. This cultural narrative plays a significant role in conservation efforts, as it highlights the intrinsic value of preserving the myths and stories tied to natural landscapes. As cryptozoology enthusiasts share these narratives, they contribute to a larger conversation about the importance of protecting the environments that inspire such legends. The intersections of culture, science, and conservation create a rich tapestry that not only honors the past but also secures the future of these enigmatic creatures.

Incorporating artistic interpretations and illustrations of Cadborosaurus into conservation campaigns can also enhance public engagement. Visual representations have the power to evoke emotions and spark curiosity, driving interest in marine conservation. By collaborating with artists and filmmakers, conservationists can create compelling narratives that highlight the importance of preserving coastal habitats. Documentaries focusing on Cadborosaurus can further amplify these efforts, reaching a broader audience and emphasizing the need for collective action. Ultimately, the integration of art, science, and community engagement is key to ensuring that both Cadborosaurus and its environment are protected for future generations.

CHAPTER 10

Documentary Filmmaking Focused on Cadborosaurus

Notable Documentaries and Their Impact

Documentaries have played a crucial role in shaping public perception and understanding of cryptids like Cadborosaurus. Through a blend of expert interviews, eyewitness accounts, and stunning visuals, notable documentaries have brought the mystery of this elusive sea creature to the forefront of cryptozoological discussions. These films not only captivate audiences but also provide a platform for scientific inquiry and debate, allowing viewers to engage with the evidence and theories surrounding Cadborosaurus. The impact of these documentaries extends beyond mere entertainment, fostering a deeper appreciation for the unexplained phenomena of our oceans.

One of the most significant documentaries featuring Cadborosaurus is "The Beast of Cadborosaurus," which explores the myriad sightings along the Pacific Coast and presents firsthand accounts from local residents. This film emphasizes the importance of eyewitness testimony in the study of cryptids, showcasing interviews with individuals who claim to have encountered the creature. By presenting these personal stories, the documentary humanizes the search for Cadborosaurus, encouraging viewers to consider the validity of experiences that often go dismissed by mainstream science. The emotional resonance of these accounts can inspire further interest in the ongoing search for evidence of the creature's existence.

The scientific aspect of Cadborosaurus has also been highlighted in various documentaries, which delve into the biological and ecological implications of such a creature inhabiting coastal waters. These films often feature marine biologists and cryptozoologists who discuss the potential habitats and environmental factors that could support the existence of Cadborosaurus. By incorporating scientific theories and research into the narrative, these documentaries aim to bridge the gap between folklore and science, prompting viewers to consider how traditional stories may inform contemporary understanding of marine biology. The blending of science with storytelling enriches the documentary experience and encourages critical thinking among viewers.

In addition to factual presentations, some documentaries have embraced artistic interpretations of Cadborosaurus, showcasing illustrations and animations that bring the creature to life. These visual representations can significantly impact audience perception, as they provide a tangible image of what Cadborosaurus could look like based on descriptions from historical accounts and eyewitness reports. Artistic portrayals can spark imagination and curiosity, inviting audiences to visualize the creature in the context of its supposed habitat. Such creative elements help to maintain interest in Cadborosaurus and its lore, ensuring that the search for this cryptid remains a vibrant part of popular culture.

Ultimately, the impact of notable documentaries on the narrative surrounding Cadborosaurus extends beyond mere fascination. They serve as a catalyst for discussion within the cryptozoology community, encouraging enthusiasts to share their own experiences and engage with ongoing research. By highlighting both the mysteries and the scientific inquiries related to Cadborosaurus, these films foster a culture of exploration and inquiry that is essential to the field of cryptozoology. As viewers become more informed about the complexities surrounding this enigmatic creature, the quest for truth continues, fueled by curiosity and a desire to uncover the secrets lurking beneath the waves.

Techniques Used in Cryptid Documentaries

Techniques used in cryptid documentaries often blend a variety of storytelling methods and visual strategies to engage viewers while presenting the enigmatic nature of creatures like Cadborosaurus. One prevalent approach is the use of dramat reenactments, which aim to bring eyewitness accounts to life. By casting actors to portray witnesses and utilizing cinematic techniques, filmmakers can create a vivid narrative that draws audiences into the mystery of Cadborosaurus sightings. These reenactments, while sometimes criticized for lacking authenticity, serve to illustrate the emotional weight of the testimonies, making them more relatable for viewers.

Interviews with experts and enthusiasts form another vital component of cryptid documentaries. Filmmakers frequently seek out marine biologists, cryptozoologists, and local historians to provide context and credibility to the discussions surrounding Cadborosaurus. These interviews can offer scientific perspectives on the creature's potential existence, as well as insights into the folklore and regional lore surrounding its sightings. By incorporating multiple viewpoints, documentaries not only enrich the narrative but also encourage viewers to consider different angles of the ongoing debate about Cadborosaurus.

Visual elements play a crucial role in conveying the allure of cryptids. Drone footage, underwater cameras, and high-quality graphics are commonly used to explore the habitats associated with Cadborosaurus. This technique not only enhances the aesthetic appeal of the documentary but also serves to highlight the environmental conditions that may support the existence of such a creature. By visually immersing the audience in the coastal landscapes of potential Cadborosaurus sightings, filmmakers can evoke a sense of wonder and curiosity, prompting viewers to ponder the mysteries that lie beneath the waves.

Furthermore, sound design is an often-overlooked aspect of cryptid documentaries that can significantly impact viewer engagement. Ambient sounds, such as ocean waves, distant animal calls, and eerie music, can heighten suspense and create an immersive atmosphere. These auditory cues are carefully crafted to evoke emotions and set the tone for various segments, whether they are discussing historical accounts, scientific investigations, or popular culture representations of Cadborosaurus. The right soundscape can intensify the viewer's experience, drawing them deeper into the narrative.

Finally, the integration of archival footage and graphics is a technique that lends credibility and historical context to cryptid documentaries. By showcasing old photographs, newspaper clippings, and maps, filmmakers can trace the lineage of Cadborosaurus sightings through time. This historical perspective not only informs viewers about past encounters but also situates the current search for Cadborosaurus within a broader context of human curiosity and folklore. By combining these diverse techniques, cryptid documentaries aim to captivate audiences and deepen their understanding of the enigmatic Cadborosaurus, fostering a sense of connection to the ongoing exploration of this elusive creature.

The Future of Documentary Filmmaking in Cryptozoology

The future of documentary filmmaking in the realm of cryptozoology, particularly concerning Cadborosaurus, holds exciting potential for both enthusiasts and researchers. As technology continues to evolve, filmmakers now have access to advanced tools and techniques that can enhance storytelling and visualization. High-quality underwater drones, 360-degree cameras, and augmented reality applications can provide immersive experiences that bring the elusive Cadborosaurus to life. These innovations allow for the exploration of the habitats and environments where sightings have occurred, providing a more detailed context for viewers and researchers alike.

Documentaries focusing on Cadborosaurus are increasingly incorporating scientific studies and eyewitness accounts to bolster their narratives. By blending personal testimonies with rigorous scientific inquiry, filmmakers can create a compelling case that invites viewers to consider the possibility of cryptids beyond mere folklore. Engaging interviews with researchers, historians, and eyewitnesses can paint a multifaceted picture of the creature's lore, while expert analyses can provide a critical lens through which to interpret the evidence. This hybrid approach not only educates audiences but also fosters a sense of community among those who share a fascination with the mysteries of the natural world.

The portrayal of Cadborosaurus in popular culture and media has also begun to influence the documentary landscape. As interest in cryptids grows, filmmakers are tapping into the rich history of Cadborosaurus sightings and integrating elements of folklore into their narratives. This not only serves to entertain but also to preserve the cultural significance of the creature within coastal communities. By examining historical accounts alongside modern encounters, documentaries can highlight the continuity of the Cadborosaurus mythos and its evolving representation in media, appealing to both skeptics and believers.

Artistic interpretations and illustrations of Cadborosaurus are another critical aspect that filmmakers can leverage to enhance their documentaries. Collaborating with artists to create visual representations can bring a level of creativity and imagination that transcends traditional documentary formats. These visuals can help bridge the gap between scientific inquiry and the artistic expression of cryptozoology, making the subject matter more accessible and engaging. By incorporating these illustrations, filmmakers can evoke the wonder and mystery surrounding Cadborosaurus, prompting viewers to explore the depths of their own curiosity.

Lastly, as environmental concerns become increasingly pressing, documentaries that address the ecological impact on Cadborosaurus habitats may play a pivotal role in advocacy and awareness. By examining how changes in marine ecosystems might influence sightings or the existence of Cadborosaurus, filmmakers can present a compelling case for conservation efforts. This approach not only emphasizes the importance of protecting the natural world but also invites viewers to consider the broader implications of their own relationship with nature. As filmmakers continue to explore these themes, the future of documentary filmmaking in cryptozoology will undoubtedly inspire new generations to engage with the mysteries that lie beneath the waves.

CHAPTER 11

Conclusion

The Ongoing Mystery of Cadborosaurus

The Cadborosaurus, often referred to simply as "Caddy," continues to captivate the imaginations of cryptozoologists and enthusiasts alike. This elusive sea serpent is chiefly reported in the coastal waters of British Columbia, particularly in the Strait of Georgia. Eyewitness accounts, dating back to the late 19th century, describe a long, serpentine creature with a horse-like head, often attributed to the mysterious depths of the ocean. As interest in Caddy has persisted, the ongoing mystery surrounding its existence has prompted both amateur and professional researchers to investigate the nuances of various sightings and their implications for marine biology.

Eyewitness accounts of Cadborosaurus vary widely, with some claiming to have seen the creature breach the water's surface, revealing its elongated body and distinctive features. Others recount instances of seeing multiple humps or a large tail. These reports often evoke a sense of wonder and skepticism, as they challenge the boundaries of what is considered scientifically valid. Cryptozoologists have compiled databases of sightings, analyzing the details and contexts in which these encounters occur. While some witnesses have been discredited or dismissed as unreliable, others present compelling narratives that deserve further investigation.

Scientific studies and theories regarding Cadborosaurus often delve into the possibility of misidentified marine animals. Some researchers propose that sightings could be attributed to known species, such as sea lions or large fish, which may exhibit unusual behaviors or appearances under certain conditions. Others entertain the prospect that Caddy represents an undiscovered species, potentially a prehistoric survivor or a cousin to known sea creatures. This notion prompts discussions about the ecological roles that such a creature could play and the environmental conditions necessary for its survival.

The allure of Cadborosaurus extends beyond the realm of cryptozoology and into popular culture and media. Documentaries and fictional portrayals, ranging from films to literature, often depict Caddy as a symbol of the unknown lurking just beneath the surface. These representations can shape public perception, influencing both the interest in and skepticism surrounding the creature. Artistic interpretations, whether through paintings or digital art, further contribute to the mystique, inviting viewers to envision what this enigmatic being might look like and where it might reside.

Historical accounts and folklore also play a crucial role in shaping the narrative of Cadborosaurus. Indigenous stories often speak of sea serpents and other mythical creatures, suggesting a long-standing cultural acknowledgment of such beings in the region. Comparisons between Cadborosaurus and other legendary sea monsters, such as the Loch Ness Monster or the Ogopogo, reveal common themes in myth and the human fascination with the ocean's mysteries. As environmental factors continue to influence habitats along the coast, understanding the potential impacts on the ecosystem is essential for future research. The ongoing mystery of Cadborosaurus remains a testament to humanity's enduring quest to uncover the secrets of the natural world.

Implications for Cryptozoology

The study of Cadborosaurus brings with it a host of implications for the broader field of cryptozoology. This enigmatic sea creature, often described as a serpent-like entity inhabiting the coastal waters of the Pacific Northwest, has captivated the imagination of enthusiasts and researchers alike. The pursuit of understanding Cadborosaurus not only challenges the boundaries of established scientific knowledge but also ignites discussions about the validity of eyewitness accounts and the role of folklore in shaping our perceptions of cryptids. Each reported sighting contributes to a growing tapestry of narratives that demand careful analysis and open-minded exploration.

Eyewitness accounts play a pivotal role in the ongoing investigation into Cadborosaurus. Many enthusiasts find themselves drawn to the nuances of these testimonies, which often vary widely in detail and emotional resonance. While skeptics may dismiss such accounts as mere fantasy or misidentification, proponents argue that these narratives can offer valuable insights into the creature's behavior and habitat. By compiling and scrutinizing these reports, researchers can identify patterns that may lead to a deeper understanding of Cadborosaurus and its ecological niche, further legitimizing the field of cryptozoology as a legitimate area of study.

Scientific studies and theories surrounding Cadborosaurus also influence our understanding of cryptozoology. Investigative efforts often involve interdisciplinary approaches, drawing from marine biology, ecology, and anthropology to piece together a comprehensive picture of how such a creature might exist. The possibility of undiscovered marine species lends credence to the search for Cadborosaurus, prompting scientists to explore oceanic environments long considered inhospitable or devoid of life. This exploration not only fuels cryptozoological inquiry but also has broader implications for marine conservation efforts and the understanding of biodiversity.

The portrayal of Cadborosaurus in popular culture and media has further enriched the discourse surrounding this cryptid. Documentaries, films, and literature have contributed to the mythos, often blending fact with fiction in ways that both inspire and mislead. Artistic interpretations and illustrations serve to visualize the creature, shaping public perception and generating interest in the search for evidence. As media representations evolve, they reflect and influence societal attitudes toward cryptozoology, sometimes fostering a sense of wonder while also raising questions about the line between reality and myth.

Finally, the environmental impact on Cadborosaurus habitats provides critical context for its search. The degradation of marine ecosystems due to climate change, pollution, and overfishing poses significant threats to any undiscovered species that may inhabit these waters. Understanding the ecological factors that could affect the survival of Cadborosaurus not only enriches the narrative of its existence but also emphasizes the importance of conservation. As cryptozoologists pursue answers about this elusive creature, they simultaneously advocate for the preservation of its environment, illustrating the interconnectedness of cryptozoology with broader ecological concerns.

The Future of the Search for Cadborosaurus

The future of the search for Cadborosaurus holds an intriguing promise, blending scientific inquiry with the allure of folklore and popular culture. As cryptozoology continues to capture the imagination of enthusiasts, the pursuit of Cadborosaurus—an enigmatic sea creature reputedly inhabiting the waters off the Pacific Northwest—will likely benefit from advancements in technology and methodology. The integration of remote sensing technologies, such as underwater drones and advanced sonar systems, could significantly enhance the ability to explore the depths where this creature might dwell. These tools offer unprecedented opportunities to survey large marine areas, mapping out habitats that align with historical sightings and eyewitness accounts.

As the scientific community increasingly embraces interdisciplinary approaches, collaboration between cryptozoologists, marine biologists, and historians could lead to more robust studies of Cadborosaurus. By examining historical accounts and folklore alongside modern scientific methods, researchers can create a comprehensive narrative that respects the cultural significance of these sightings while seeking evidence. Peer-reviewed studies focused on environmental impacts, such as climate change and pollution, are crucial in understanding how these factors may influence Cadborosaurus habitats and sightings. This multifaceted approach could stimulate further interest in the subject, as well as foster a more serious discourse surrounding the existence of this cryptid.

Public interest in Cadborosaurus remains strong, fueled by its presence in popular media and culture. Documentaries and films that spotlight the search for this creature can capture a wider audience, igniting curiosity and inspiring amateur researchers to contribute to the quest. These visual narratives not only serve to entertain but also educate viewers on the complexities of cryptozoology and the challenges faced by those seeking to prove the existence of elusive creatures. As filmmakers delve into the mystique of Cadborosaurus, they have the opportunity to highlight both the scientific and mythological aspects of the search, bridging the gap between fact and fiction.

Artistic interpretations of Cadborosaurus play a pivotal role in shaping public perception and sparking interest in its lore. Illustrations and reconstructions based on eyewitness accounts can help visualize the creature, making it more tangible for enthusiasts and casual observers alike. These artistic endeavors can be instrumental in keeping the story of Cadborosaurus alive, reminding audiences of the intersection between art, myth, and science. As new sightings and testimonies emerge, artists can further refine their representations, reflecting the evolving narrative surrounding this elusive sea monster.

Ultimately, the future of the search for Cadborosaurus hinges on a blend of technology, community engagement, and continued exploration of its environmental context. As cryptozoologists and enthusiasts unite in their quest, the possibility of uncovering tangible evidence becomes increasingly feasible. The coexistence of scientific rigor with the rich tapestry of folklore ensures that the pursuit remains vibrant and relevant. Whether Cadborosaurus is eventually classified as a new species or remains a part of cryptozoological lore, the journey itself enriches our understanding of the mysteries that lie beneath the waves.